THE WORRY (LESS) BOOK

FEEL STRONG, FIND CALM AND TAME YOUR ANXIETY!

SEE YOU LATER!

RACHEL BRIAN

wren & rook

FOR ENZO, THE BRAVE, WHO EMBRACES HIS ANXIETY
WITH THE WARM HUG OF ACCEPTANCE.
THOUGH NEVER VANQUISHED, ANXIETY
NEVER STOPS HIM FROM FOLLOWING HIS HEART.

First published in the UK in 2020 by Wren & Rook
Simultaneously published in the US in 2020 by Hachette
Book Group

Text and illustration copyright © Rachel Brian, 2020
Cover copyright © 2020 by Hodder & Stoughton Limited

Cover design by Laura Hambleton and Karina Granda
Edited by Lisa Yoskowitz and Laura Horsley

All rights reserved

The right of Rachel Brian to be identified as the author/
illustrator respectively of this Work has been asserted by
her in accordance with the Copyright, Designs & Patents
Act 1988.

ISBN: 978 1526 36278 0
E-book ISBN: 978 1526 36293 3
10 9 8 7 6 5 4 3 2 1

MIX
Paper from
responsible sources
FSC
www.fsc.org
FSC® C104740

Wren & Rook
An imprint of
Hachette Children's Group
Part of Hodder & Stoughton
Carmelite House
50 Victoria Embankment
London EC4Y 0DZ

An Hachette UK Company
www.hachette.co.uk
www.hachettechildrens.co.uk

Printed in China

X075105

Community Learning & Libraries
Cymuned Ddysgu a Llyfrgelloedd

Newport
CITY COUNCIL
CYNGOR DINAS
Casnewydd

This item should be returned or renewed by the last date stamped below.

Pihi.

-- 2 MAR 2022	-------------------	-------------------
-------------------	-------------------	-------------------
-------------------	-------------------	-------------------
-------------------	-------------------	-------------------
-------------------	-------------------	-------------------
-------------------	-------------------	-------------------
-------------------	-------------------	-------------------
-------------------	-------------------	-------------------
-------------------	-------------------	-------------------
-------------------	-------------------	-------------------

To renew visit:

www.newport.gov.uk/libraries

WELCOME!

THIS BOOK IS FOR PEOPLE WHO WORRY.
SO, YEAH, EVERYONE!

WHAT THIS BOOK **CAN** DO:

EXPLAIN HOW YOUR BODY REACTS TO WORRIES.

AM I SICK?

(NOPE.)

HELP YOU RECOGNISE ANXIETY.

THERE IT IS!

Ahh ...

GIVE YOU IDEAS FOR CALMING YOURSELF.

WHAT IT **CAN'T** DO:

TELL YOU **HOW TO** WORRY.

THAT COMES NATURALLY.

PICK UP YOUR DIRTY SOCKS.

NO WAY!

MAKE ALL ANXIETY DISAPPEAR.

BUMMER.

WAIT, WHAT'S ANXIETY?

ANXIETY IS A FEELING,

JUST LIKE  JOY OR ANGER OR HOPE.

IT'S THE FEELING OF BEING

Aaah!

WORRIED, NERVOUS OR AFRAID.

ANXIETY CAN ALERT US TO A THREAT.

LOOK OUT!

THANKS!

DANGER!

ANXIETY

BUT IT CAN ALSO FEEL VERY **UNCOMFORTABLE!**

UGH.

ANXIETY

4

SO WHETHER YOU HAVE:

A LITTLE ANXIETY ABOUT A FEW THINGS (OR) A LOT OF ANXIETY ABOUT A WHOLE HEAP OF THINGS,

GETTING CALLED ON IN CLASS

MEAN DOGS

CANTEEN FOOD

BUS RIDES

ANY DOGS!

CONCERTS AND PERFORMANCES

MAKING NEW FRIENDS

...IES

MATHS TESTS

THIS BOOK IS HERE TO HELP YOU:

UNDERSTAND YOUR ANXIETY,

I GET YOU!

AW!

ANXIETY

RECOGNISE IT'S A NORMAL PART OF LIFE,

OH, HI AGAIN.

HEY.

FIND TOOLS TO FEEL CALMER.

SEE YA!

TOOLBOX

chapter 1 YOUR BODY'S ALARM SYSTEM

EVERYONE HAS A MIX OF FUN AND NOT-SO-FUN FEELINGS EACH DAY:

7.00AM TOOTHPASTE EXPLODES — GRR. — **ANNOYED**

9.00AM FRIENDS! — **EXCITED**

1.00PM EXAM — OH NO. — **STRESSED**

3.00PM FOOTBALL — **CONFIDEN**

AND **EVERYONE**

FEELS ANXIOUS SOMETIMES.

I'M ANXIOUS RIGHT NOW!

ANXIETY IS LIKE YOUR BODY'S OWN ALARM SYSTEM — IT ALERTS YOU TO DANGER.

SOMETIMES THE ALARM GOES OFF BECAUSE YOUR BRAIN **PREDICTS** THAT A SITUATION MIGHT BE DANGEROUS.

THERE ARE DIFFERENT WAYS ANXIETY SHOWS UP ...

YOU MIGHT FEEL:

UNEASY
(GENERALLY LIKE THINGS AREN'T OK.)

FEARFUL
(AFRAID SOMETHING IS DANGEROUS.)

NERVOUS
(RESTLESS, JUMPY, ON EDGE.)

WORRIED
(OCCUPIED WITH IMAGINING FUTURE PROBLEMS.)

STRESSED
(TENSE AND OVERWHELMED.)

PANICKED
(SUDDENLY INTENSELY FEARFUL.)

THOUGH IT MIGHT NOT ALWAYS BE WELCOME, SOME ANXIETY CAN BE HELPFUL:

THE PREDICTIONS YOUR BRAIN MAKES CAN KEEP YOU SAFE.

BUT **TOO MUCH** ANXIETY CAN GET IN THE WAY:

 MATHS TEST THIS FRIDAY. ALERT!

 EEP!

 OH NO OH NO OH NO NO NO!

 I'M DOOMED!

 TEST!! NO NO NO.

 THIS IS THE WORST JUST LIKE I THOUGHT!

| SUNDAY | MONDAY | TUESDAY | WEDNESDAY | THURSDAY | FRIDAY |

SOME ANXIETIES AREN'T HELPFUL ...

 I'M AFRAID OF SNOW!

ESPECIALLY IF THE THING YOU'RE WORRIED ABOUT ISN'T REALLY A PROBLEM.

BUT WE LIVE ON A TROPICAL ISLAND!

GOOD POINT. BUT I STILL FEEL WORRIED.

OK, SO I'M NOT PERFECT!

10

SOMETIMES ANXIETY DOESN'T HAVE A FOCUS AND THERE'S NOTHING IN PARTICULAR YOU'RE WORRIED ABOUT.

OTHER TIMES, THERE'S A CAUSE FOR YOUR ANXIETY, BUT YOU'RE JUST NOT SURE WHAT IT IS.

YOU DON'T GET TO PICK WHAT YOU WORRY ABOUT OR WHEN.

SOME PEOPLE NATURALLY WORRY MORE STRONGLY OR MORE OFTEN THAN OTHER PEOPLE.

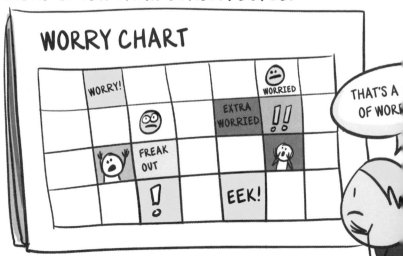

AND HOW MUCH ANXIETY YOU FEEL GOES UP AND DOWN.

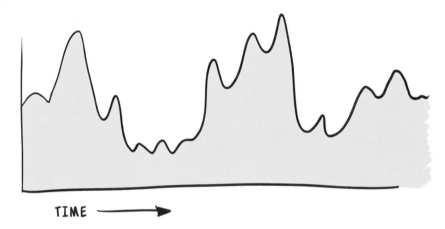

TIME ⟶

UT THERE'S NO 'RIGHT' OR 'WRONG' AMOUNT.

YOU FEEL WHAT YOU FEEL!

OCCASIONALLY, PEOPLE FEEL A STRONG, SUDDEN FEELING OF ANXIETY CALLED **PANIC.**

I'VE HAD THAT!

IT MIGHT BE A SENSE OF OVERWHELMING DREAD,

≥Gulp≥

OR IT MIGHT FEEL TOTALLY PHYSICAL.

OW! CHEST PAIN!

BUT DON'T WORRY — EVEN REALLY POWERFUL FEELINGS LIKE PANIC WON'T HURT YOU PHYSICALLY.

IT'S JUST A WHOLE BUNCH OF ME!

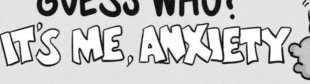

chapter 2

GUESS WHO?

IT'S ME, ANXIETY

Helloooo!!

IF YOU AREN'T SURE WHAT THEY ARE,
ANXIOUS FEELINGS CAN BE UNSETTLING.

EEK!

BUT WHEN YOU CAN RECOGNISE YOUR ANXIETY —
IT'S NOT SO SCARY.

OH, HI.
YOU AGAIN.

HI!

JUST A
SHADOW.

HI, MY NAME IS
Anxiety

15

SOMETIMES ANXIETY SHOWS UP IN YOUR THOUGHTS,

ESPECIALLY IF YOU'RE WORRIED ABOUT A SPECIFIC EVENT

BUT SOME THOUGHTS ARE FREQUENT, INTENSE AND DON'T GO AWAY AFTER A STRESSFUL EXPERIENCE.

SOMETIMES ANXIETY SHOWS UP IN THE WAY YOU FEEL.

YOU MIGHT FEEL ONE, NONE OR ALL OF THESE!

WHAT ANXIETY DOES IN YOUR **BODY**

YOUR BODY RELEASES
ADRENALINE
(A STRESS HORMONE).

IT MAKES YOU BREATHE FASTER AND QUICKENS YOUR HEART RATE. IT'S GREAT IF YOU NEED TO FLEE FROM AN ANGRY RACCOON!

BUT IT'S NOT GREAT IF YOU'RE TRYING TO FEEL CALM OR FALL ASLEEP.

NXIETY CAN MAKE YOU FEEL LIKE
METHING IS **TERRIBLY WRONG** ...

WHO ME?!
SORRY ABOUT
THAT!

FEELING ANXIOUS?

YEAH! IT'S **SCARY**!

THAT'S YOUR BODY'S
NATURAL RESPONSE.
IT FEELS AWFUL,
BUT YOU'RE OK!

I'M OK? ≳PHEW!≲

UT KNOW THAT THE
AD FEELING WILL
GO AWAY WITH TIME.

YAY! WAIT ...
HOW MUCH TIME?

WELL, I'VE GOT LUNCH
PLANS AT 1.00 ...

SOMETIMES JUST KNOWING YOUR ANXIETY IS
TEMPORARY AND NOT DANGEROUS CAN HELP.

I KNOW I'M
GOING TO BE
FINE.

TIME

Ahhh...

PEOPLE HAVE LOTS OF **REACTIONS** TO ANXIETY:

GETTING ANGRY

NEEDING DISTRACTION

REDOING WORK

CRAVING REASSURANCE

EATING WHEN NOT HUNGRY

AVOIDING DAILY LIFE

FEELING SICK

TRYING NOT TO CARE ABOUT ANYTHING.

THE MORE YOU CAN RECOGNISE ANXIETY
(IN ALL ITS DISGUISES,)

THE MORE YOU CAN DEAL WITH IT DIRECTL
WHEN YOU'RE READY TO.

NEWS FLASH

YOU MIGHT BE WONDERING:

> IF ANXIETY IS NATURAL AND USEFUL, WHY DO I HAVE SO MANY UNHELPFUL WORRIES?

WELL, WHILE NATURE HAS CREATED MANY COOL AND USEFUL ADAPTATIONS SUCH AS:

SEEING IS GREAT!

EYES

I'M CUTE AND TOASTY!

FUR COATS

I CAN OPEN A JAR!

OPPOSABLE THUMBS

SOME NATURAL THINGS CAN MAKE LIFE A BIT TOUGHER:

MESMERISING!

DEER BEHAVIOUR ON ROADS

OW! MY APPENDIX!

THE APPENDIX

OH NO! I'M FLYING INTO THAT CANDLE AGAIN!

MOTH NAVIGATION

SO ... YEAH — YOUR ANXIETY IS NATURAL, BUT IT CAN ALSO BE CHALLENGING.

chapter 3

WORRY IN THE WAY

EEP.

NOW YOU KNOW HOW TO

RECOGNISE ANXIETY.

(GOOD JOB!)

HEY! THERE IT IS!!

WHO, ME?

NOW IT'S TIME TO FIGURE OUT IF IT'S

IN YOUR WAY.

OHH ... AM I IN YOUR WAY?

YUP.

HI, MY NAME IS
Anxiety

LIFE, THIS WAY!

OW DO YOU KNOW IF ANXIETY IS CAUSING PROBLEM?

ASK YOURSELF:
AM I DOING WHAT'S IMPORTANT TO ME?

IF YOU'RE FEELING A LOT OF ANXIETY, A LOT OF THE TIME — IT CAN BE HARD TO DO THE THINGS YOU WANT TO.

YOU MIGHT FIND IT'S CAUSING PROBLEMS WITH

SLEEP

ONE OF THE BEST WAYS TO TELL IF ANXIETY IS A PROBLEM FOR YOU IS TO LOOK AT WHAT YOU

IF YOU'RE AVOIDING THINGS LIKE:

THEN YOU MIGHT BE EXPERIENCING A LOT OF ANXIET

THE FARTY PARTY

A MINI-COMIC ABOUT 'WHAT IF'?

SOMETIMES THE WORST THING IMAGINABLE TURNS
OUT TO BE NO BIG DEAL.

chapter 4

FEEL LIKE POO?
TAKE CARE of YOU!

YEAH!

IF ANXIETY IS GETTING YOU DOWN, YOU MIGHT NEED SOME TOOLS TO CALM YOURSELF AND HELP YOU GET UNSTUCK.

THESE TOOLS CAN GO IN YOUR ANXIETY **TOOLBOX.**

LIKE THESE?

UH, NO. NOT LITERAL TOOLS.

STRATEGIES TO HELP YOU FEEL OK EVEN WHEN YOU HAVE ANXIETY!

IDEAS THIS WAY

START WITH

THE BASICS.

OK, YOU'RE NOT FEELING GREAT.

BUT THERE MAY BE A FEW THINGS THAT CAN HELP.

YOUR BODY IS A BIT LIKE A HOUSE PLANT.

IT IS?

YEP.

IF YOU TAKE CARE OF PLANTS, THEY DO PRETTY WELL:

AND IF YOU DON'T, THEY DON'T DO SO WELL:

IT'S THE SAME THING WITH YOUR BODY.

IT NEEDS SOME BASIC THINGS TO FEEL GOOD.
AND WITHOUT THOSE THINGS ...

EVERYONE IS DIFFERENT WHEN IT COMES TO WHAT MAKES THEM FEEL GOOD.

BUT WHEN YOU FEEL BAD, ASK YOURSELF:

COULD I FEEL BETTER IF I TOOK TIME TO ...

SCIENCE CORNER

WHY DO SIMPLE THINGS SOMETIMES HELP?

ALERT!

WHEN YOU'RE TIRED, HUNGRY, THIRSTY, TOO HOT OR TOO COLD, YOUR BODY CAN TELL SOMETHING'S OFF.

THAT TRIGGERS YOUR BRAIN'S ALARM SYSTEM.

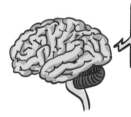

BEGIN OPERATION FREAK OUT!

Ahh.

IF YOU CAN SOOTHE YOUR BODY A BIT, SOMETIMES YOUR BRAIN CAN RELAX TOO.

FALSE ALARM? COOL! LET'S CHILL.

WANTED

FOR MAKING ANXIETY WORSE

CAFFEINE

TOO MUCH SUGAR

LOADS OF SCREEN TIME

BEWARE OF THIS NOTORIOUS GANG!

THE **REWARD** FOR LIMITING YOUR CONTACT WITH THESE CULPRITS —

FEELING MORE RELAXED.

OK, SO IF YOU'VE DONE ALL THAT AND YOU **STILL** FEEL ANXIOUS ...

NOW I'M FULL OF SANDWICH AND ANXIETY!

IT'S TIME TO LOOK AT SOME SPECIFIC TOOLS TO HELP CALM AND RELAX YOU.

OOOH! I FOUND A SPANNER!

≷SIGH.≷ IT'S A METAPHOR!

chapter 5

TRAIN YOUR BRAIN

SIT. STAY! GOOD BRAIN!

OK, YOU CAN'T REALLY CONTROL YOUR BRAIN.

BRAIN, FORGET THAT EMBARRASSING INCIDENT WITH THE UNDERWEAR.

NOPE.

STOP BEING ANXIOUS RIGHT NOW!

UH-UH.

HAVE ONLY HAPPY EMOTIONS!

NOT GONNA DO IT.

JUST LIKE YOU CAN'T CONTROL A LOT OF WHAT YOUR BODY DOES.

STOP THAT DIGESTING RIGHT NOW.

NO SWEATING!

UGH.

HI, MY NAME IS
Anxiety

BUT WHEN YOU'RE KNEE-DEEP IN ANXIETY, THERE ARE SOME THINGS YOU CAN DO THAT MAY HELP YOUR MIND AND BODY GET BACK IN BALANCE.

WHEEEE!

THEY'RE STRATEGIES YOU CAN KEEP IN YOUR ANXIETY TOOLBOX...

SOME ARE WAYS TO CALM YOURSELF WHEN YOUR ANXIETY IS HIGH. OTHERS ARE IDEAS FOR STAYING RESILIENT AND STRONG.

TOOL #1 BREATHING

FOCUS ON THE FEELING OF YOUR BREATH AS IT GOES IN AND OUT.

HOW IT WORKS: SLOW BREATHING

ANXIETY IS LIKE A CAR GAS PEDAL.

BREATHING FASTER

RELEASES ADRENALINE!

SPEEDS UP HEART RATE!

MORE NERVOUS AND JITTERY

SLOW BREATHING IS LIKE THE BRAKES.

STIMULATES THE VAGUS NERVE. (THAT'S GOOD!)

HEART RATE SLOWS

Ahhh.

CALMER AND MORE RELAXED

41

TOOL #2 GROUNDING YOUR BODY

 START → **NOTICE 5 THINGS YOU SEE.**

LIKE ...
- THE WINDOW
- YELLOW RUG
- MY HANDS
- A FLY
- OLD PLASTER

NOTICE 1 THING YOU TASTE

- TODAY'S SANDWICH (TUNA!).

- A PILLOW
- THE GROUND
- THE AIR
- SAME OLD PLASTER

NOTICE 4 THINGS YOU CAN TOUCH.

- A PENCIL
- MY SOCKS (EW!).

NOTICE 2 THINGS YOU SMELL.

- A BIRD
- MY BREATHING
- SOMEONE BURPING.

NOTICE 3 THINGS YOU HEAR.

HOW IT WORKS:

WHEN YOU'RE ANXIOUS, YOUR MIND MAY BE AGITATED OR HAVE UNSETTLING THOUGHTS.

WHEN YOU FOCUS ON YOUR BODY AND SENSES INSTEAD, IT GIVES YOUR MIND A CHANCE TO QUIETEN DOWN.

 THANKS FOR THE BREAK!

TOOL #3
KEEP A WORRY JOURNAL

WRITE DOWN ALL
THE THINGS YOU'RE
WORRIED ABOUT.

...CAN
...RE
...R
...T WITH
...PPORTIVE
...END
...ADULT.

YOU CAN EVEN
PLAN TO LOOK
AT YOUR
WORRIES LATER.
SOMETIMES THAT
CAN HELP YOU
RELAX.

TO THINK
ABOUT
TOMORROW

HOW IT WORKS:

WHEN YOU LOOK RIGHT
AT THEM, THE WORRIES
DON'T SEEM AS SCARY.

HI THERE.

YO.

TOOL #4
MUSCLE
RELAXATION

1 LIE DOWN AND BREATHE SLOWLY.

2 STARTING WITH YOUR TOES — SQUEEZE THEM AS HARD AS YOU CAN FOR TEN SECONDS.

4 DON'T FORGET YOUR BELLY, EYELIDS AND EVERYTHING IN BETWEEN! (YES, EVEN YOUR BUM!)

THEN LET THEM RELAX FOR TEN SECONDS.

3 MOVE YOUR WAY UP YOUR BODY, SQUEEZING EACH MUSCLE AS HARD AS YOU CAN AND THEN LETTING IT RELAX.

HOW IT WORKS:

WHEN YOU'RE ANXIOUS, YOUR MUSCLES ARE OFTEN TIGHT AND TENSE. DOING THIS ACTIVITY MAKES EACH MUSCLE GROUP RELAX.

CHILL OUT.

TOOL #5
VISUALISATION

IF YOUR MIND IS RACING WITH
UNCOMFORTABLE THOUGHTS,
TRY IMAGINING YOURSELF IN A
RELAXING PLACE.

IAT DOES IT LOOK LIKE?

WHAT DOES IT SOUND LIKE?

IAT DOES IT FEEL LIKE?

WHAT DOES IT SMELL LIKE?

HOW IT WORKS:

WHEN YOU IMAGINE SOMETHING,
YOUR BRAIN INTERPRETS IT AS THOUGH IT'S
REAL. THINKING ABOUT A RELAXING PLACE
HELPS YOUR BRAIN RELAX TOO.

TOOL #6
CHALLENGING NEGATIVE THOUGHTS

JUST BECAUSE YOU HAVE A THOUGHT...   DOESN'T MAKE IT TRUE.

WE'RE DOOMED! DOOMED, I TELL YOU!

WE'RE FINE, REALLY!

SO WHEN YOU HAVE A NEGATIVE THOUGHT, ASK YOURSELF TWO QUESTIONS:

1 HOW LIKELY IS IT TO HAPPEN?

2 WHAT'S THE WORST TH COULD HAPPEN AND HO WOULD I HANDLE IT?

HOW IT WORKS:

KNOWING YOUR WORRY IS PROBABLY UNLIKELY — AND KNOWING THAT YOU'D BE ABLE TO HANDLE WHATEVER HAPPENS ANYWAY — CAN LESSEN ANXIETY AND GIVE YOU CONFIDENCE.

THOSE SIX TOOLS MIGHT HELP YOU GET UNSTUCK WHEN YOU'RE FEELING ANXIOUS.

HERE ARE A COUPLE OF OTHER TOOLS YOU CAN USE EVERY DAY!

7 30 MINUTES OF EXERCISE EACH DAY CAN HELP YOUR BODY MANAGE ANXIETY.

8 TALKING WITH SUPPORTIVE PEOPLE WHO CARE ABOUT YOU.

TAKING A BREAK FROM SCREENS TO BE IN NATURE OR JUST RELAX. **9**

chapter 6
GET OUT OF THE ZONE

YOUR COMFORT ZONE THAT IS!

YOUR COMFORT ZONE IS THE FAMILIAR, RELAXE[D] PART OF YOUR LIFE.

AHH, COMFY!

SOME PEOPLE'S COMFORT ZONES ARE BIG:

LEARNING NEW SKILLS

TRYING NEW FOODS

EXPLORING

SHARING IDEAS

I THINK...

MEETING NEW PEOPLE

AND SOME PEOPLE'S ARE SMALL:

PLAYING WITH MY DOG

SEEING A MOVIE

EITHER WAY, STEPPING OUT OF YOUR COMFORT ZONE TO TRY EXCITING NEW THINGS CAN M[AKE] LIFE MORE FUN AND REWARDI[NG]

STEPPING OUT OF YOUR COMFORT ZONE CAN BE, WELL, **UNCOMFORTABLE.**

BUT USING THE TOOLS IN YOUR TOOLBOX CAN HELP YOU TAKE THE LEAP.

THE BEST WAY TO GROW YOUR COMFORT ZONE ...

IS BY DOING THINGS THAT MAKE YO **UN**COMFORTABLE.

...CAUSE THE MORE YOU DO SOMETHING, THE
...ORE YOUR MIND AND BODY GET USED TO IT.

THE BETTER YOU GET AT TOLERATING **DISCOMFORT,**

THAT WAS HARD, BUT I TRIED IT AND MADE IT THROUGH! I'M PROU OF MYSELF.

THE MORE COMFORTABLE YOU'LL BE MOST OF THE TIME.

FEELING CONFIDEN

HARVEY THE DOG

A MINI-COMIC

HARVEY THE DOG WAS CONTENT.

HE LOVED NAPPING ON HIS HUMANS,

ZZZZ

TREATS

AND BELLY RUBS.

BUT THERE WAS ONE THING HARVEY DID NOT LIKE...

the **OUTDOORS**...

NO NO NO NO!

C'MON!

THE OUTDOORS WAS FULL OF THINGS THAT WORRIED HARVEY...

EEK!

TIPPED-OVER FLOWERPOTS,

!

?

RUBBISH BINS,

THEY'LL NEVER SEE ME HERE!

?

FRIENDLY DOGS.

ONE DAY, HARVEY WAS ALARMED BY A TALL WEED BLOWING IN THE WIND.

BUT EVERY DAY, HARVEY WENT OUT. (A DOG'S GOTTA PEE.)

I'LL DO IT!

EVEN THOUGH HE WAS AFRAID,

WHAT'S THIS TERRIBLE WET STUFF?

HE EXPLORED,

MMM...GREAT SMELLS!

AND HE STARTED TO FEEL LESS AFRAID.

WELL, STILL AFRAID SOMETIMES.

HIDING, YES.

THAT WAS OK, BECAUSE SOMETIMES HE WASN'T AFRAID AT ALL.

HI, WEED!

HIS COMFORT GREW

MMM... I THINK I ATE A BEE! oh well.

AND GREW,

WHEE!

AND HE WAS FREE TO LIVE HIS BEST DOG LIFE

THE END

chapter 7

FAIL FORWARD

HUH?

THERE ARE LOTS OF THINGS THAT TRIGGER ANXIETY,
BUT MANY ANXIETIES HAVE A SIMILAR CAUSE —

FEAR OF
FAILURE.

EEK!

THE PROBLEM IS, YOU OFTEN HAVE
TO FAIL **MANY TIMES** BEFORE
YOU SUCCEED AT SOMETHING.

FIRST WORDS

GAC!

FIRST STEPS

WHOA!

FIRST TIME
TYING SHOES

FIRST TIME
PLAYING
BASKETBALL.

plunk

TAKING RISKS

TO LEARN AND GROW, SOMETIMES YOU HAVE T[O] TAKE RISKS.

RISKS? THAT DOESN'T SOUND SAFE!

NOT THE KIND OF RISKS THAT PUT YOU IN MORTAL DANGER.

(NO SWIMMING BLINDFOLDED WITH SHARKS WHILE HOLDING FISH HEADS.)

THE KIND OF RISKS THAT ARE SAFE BUT MIGHT MAKE YOU NERVOUS AT FIRST.

TRYING A NEW FOOD.

STUDYING A NEW LANGUAGE.

TAKING A DANCE CLASS.

LEARNING TO RIDE A BIKE.

A LOT OF PEOPLE TRY TO MAKE LIFE LOOK **PERFECT...**

(ESPECIALLY ONLINE.)

♥ 750

♥ 1,025

ONE MINUTE LATER

BUT THERE ARE LOTS OF DIFFICULT, ANXIOUS, SAD AND EMBARRASSING MOMENTS TOO.

I DEFINITELY DON'T POST THOSE!

WHY DON'T PEOPLE TALK MORE ABOUT **FAILURE?**

WELL, SOMETIMES, UNDER THE PILE OF ANXIETY, THERE'S A BIG WORRY.

WHEN YOU DIG DOWN, YOU'LL FIND IT.

AM I GOOD ENOUGH?

THE GOOD NEWS IS:

YES, YOU **ARE** GOOD ENOUGH!

JUST BY BEING YOU.

EVEN IF YOU ONLY HAVE ONE 'LIKE' AND IT'S YOUR MUM,

OR YOU GOT A BAD GRADE,

OR MADE A MISTAKE,

BEING IMPERFECT MAKES YOU HUMAN.

IMAGINE IF YOU **COULD** BE PERFECT — THAT WOULD BE SOOO BORING!

LETTING GO OF THE IDEA OF BEING PERFECT CAN LESSEN ANXIETY.

BECAUSE WHEN:

THINGS DON'T GO WELL ...

OR SOMEONE IS MAD AT YOU ...

OR YOU FEEL WORRIED ABOUT THE PAST OR FUTURE ...

WHAT IF?

IT MIGHT HELP TO REMEMBER: DIFFICULT STUFF IS JUST PART OF LIFE! YOU'RE STILL OK.

THIS GRADE ISN'T ME. I JUST NEED MORE PRACTICE.

SOMETIMES I MAKE MISTAKES. WE CAN WORK IT OUT.

IT'S NORMAL TO WORRY. I CAN ALSO THINK OF SOMETHING I'M GRATEFUL FOR.

chapter 8

SUPPORT

HERE
TO
HELP!

IF YOUR ANXIETY IS TOO BIG TO HANDLE ALONE, DON'T KEEP IT TO YOURSELF!

THERE ARE PEOPLE WHO CAN HELP:

THERAPISTS

PSYCHOLOGISTS

AND SOMETIMES DOCTORS WHO CAN PRESCRIBE MEDICINE.

THERE ARE ALSO LOTS OF RESOURCES:

WEBSITES
CALM.COM
MIND.ORG.UK
YOUNGMINDS.ORG.UK

I NEED SOME HELP LEARNING TO USE MY TOOLS, AND THAT'S OK!

NEWS FLASH!

NOT EVERYONE SHOWS UNDERSTANDING WHEN A PERSON IS FEELING ANXIOUS ...

C'MON, IT'S FINE!

DON'T BE SUCH A BABY.

WHAT'S THE BIG DEAL?

YOU'RE BEING SELFISH!

SOME PEOPLE MIGHT ACT FRUSTRATED, MAKE FUN, OR EVEN GET ANGRY.

HOW TO BE SUPPORTIVE:

TRY THIS INSTEAD!

⭐ LISTEN WITHOUT JUDGING

⭐ TRY TO UNDERSTAND

⭐ ASK WHAT SUPPORT THEY'D LIKE.

THAT SOUNDS REALLY HARD.

I BELIEVE IN YOU. HOW CAN I HELP?

THANKS.

IT HELPS TO HEAR YOU BELIEVE IN ME.

BEING
BRAVE
DOESN'T MEAN YOU DON'T HAVE FEAR OR ANXIETY ...

BRAVERY CAN MEAN DOING WHAT'S
IMPORTANT TO YOU
DESPITE YOUR ANXIETY.

EVERY CHALLENGE YOU OVERCOME, WHETHER BIG OR SMALL, WILL MAKE YOU STRONGER AND MORE CONFIDENT.

ACKNOWLEDGEMENTS

Thanks to Lorenzo Battaglia, who has tremendous personal insight into the world of anxiety and who shared many creative ideas. His thoughtful reading and commentary was invaluable.

For Lisa Yoskowitz, my editor, who tamed this book into linear format from a first draft that was more of an impressionist painting. Thanks for all your hard work and for pushing this book to be such a helpful resource for kids. It's so much stronger for your efforts.

For Laura Horsley, whose smart comments and fantastic title grounded this book.

To Laura Westberg, whose deep understanding and sharp mind came to my rescue as I worked out my ideas on a napkin over platanos maduros.

For my sagacious sis, whose brain and insights I borrow from time to time.

Thanks to Karina Granda and the whole team at Hachette, for making this book so, so beautiful in its final form.

Thanks to Molly Ker Hawn, agent extraordinaire, for being always brilliant.

For Elizabeth Cohen, PhD, cognitive behavior specialist, brilliant clinical psychologist and incredibly insightful practitioner, for being one of my expert readers, offering fantastic feedback and suggesting important and useful strategies for kids.

For John P. Forsyth, PhD, whose books on Acceptance and Commitment Therapy (ACT) were an inspiration. Thanks for your kind reading of these pages and thoughtful feedback on the ACT aspects. Your work around letting go of the struggle against anxiety was a key underpinning of this book.

For Angela Runder, LICSW, who has an intuitive sense of how children relate to anxiety, for your careful reading and feedback.

To Julie Talbutt, for 40 years of friendship. I'm lucky to know you.

For Lola and Milo Battaglia, you provided me with countless insights about the different ways anxiety can affect kids. Thanks for being so patient with me as I worked on this book. (Sorry about all the pizza!)

For Mike Araujo, who offered equal parts encouragement and distraction. You helped me find the balance and equanimity I needed to wrestle these ideas on to the page.

RACHEL BRIAN

feels anxious now and then, but she's OK with that because it's just a part of life! She is the founder, owner and principal animator of Blue Seat Studios and is best known for her work on *Tea Consent* and the book *Respect: Consent, Boundaries and Being in Charge of You*. A life-long artist, Rachel is a former researcher and educator. She lives in Rhode Island, US with a handful of children, a sprinkling of dogs and her partner.